© 2017 R.E.L. Dale

All rights reserved. No part of this publication may be reproduced, distributed, or transmitted in any form or by any means, including photocopying, recording, or other electronic or mechanical methods, without the prior written permission of the publisher, except in the case of brief quotations embodied in critical reviews and certain other noncommercial uses permitted by copyright law.

Book Design by R.E.L. Dale

rel.dale@yahoo.com

Preface

When asked what this book is about, which is of course the most necessary and recurring inquiry a writer is confronted with when the subject of his work is being discussed, I have found myself frustrated by my lack of ability to manufacture a satisfactory summary. This failure on my part invariably leaves both myself and the inquirer at a loss, and is a shortcoming that I have decided is a testament to two things: the first being my deeply rooted insistence upon a work of art speaking for itself, and the second being this particular work's admittedly esoteric nature—an esoteric nature that was inherent from its inception. When I started writing this book, I had little more than a vague idea as to what it would eventually become, but I knew there was something waiting to be revealed to me in and through the act of the writing process. Watching it crystalize into a definitive form from such an obscure vision has been one of my greatest joys as well as one of my most trying struggles. Now, as the work of writing is complete, and as the book's trajectory slowly becomes more and more independent of its writer, the vision has once again blurred to me, obscured by the uncertainty of what it has yet to become in the world of public analysis.

If you are reading this preface, I am going to operate under the assumption that you are also going to read the book that follows, and an explanation of what is entailed is now, thankfully, unnecessary. But in the absence of an explanation, I will leave you with a request coupled with some advice to take with you as you move forward in this intellectual excursion: I would ask you to remember that, as I mentioned, this book started off in uncertainty and then found itself along the way. As its reader, I hope that you will afford it the same patience and space in its consumption as was needed in its creation. And as for the piece of advice, I can think of nothing more fitting than this excerpt from the work of the late Lewis Carroll—

"...go on till you come to the end: then stop."

artIficial

Life and Place

Red Herring

Gomer

A Figure of Illustration

Blind Singularity: A Dialogue

Fundamental Paradox

The Empty Theater

How to Enter Heaven

To Divvy up a Stalemate

A Certain Ambiguity

The Door

Me

artIficial

It was fate, my fate and our fate; there were no two ways about it.

Our motivations were tied to a dark revelation, which became ever more crystallized in a world where thought and matter flowed effortlessly from the former to the latter and back. The idea that we called human history had become nothing more than an escape route, a fight-and-flight hybrid of clawing retreat, a primordial attempt at deliverance from eventuality. An eventuality that seemed to trail us with a ceaseless and singular motivation.

We had realized, through extrapolation, that humanity's evasive trajectory had started long before any conscious knowledge of a trailing threat had made itself known to the men and women of this world of story and logic. And this recognizable pattern of Darwinian implications coupled with an accreditation garnered from an obtuse understanding of unconscious motives was all the proof that we needed to convince ourselves of our convictions. We now knew that progress equaled hope: a progress that we couldn't stop. We couldn't stop before we knew, and we damn well couldn't stop now that we did.

It was assumed that a new kind of intelligence was needed to unburden us from this hapless futility of forced continuity. And make no mistake, it *was* a futility, but a futility that was inexorable in its relation to our individual and collective insistences, and there was no way of making those vanish into thin air—we had tried. Being that technology was the outward expression of our intellectual capabilities, a new technological paradigm was seen as the means for transcending humanity's fall into paradox. We thought it the only chance we had for a measure of liberation. A liberation that would be concurrent with avoiding the implied destruction that had set this all into motion to begin with.

Our accomplishments were initially remarkable. Life seemed more the musings of Isaac Asimov than the state of affairs previously expected of a typical Tuesday morning. The things that we created started out as novel, matured into fantastic, and finally culminated just short of perfection—just short. Something was missing, and this something missing was an absence that kept our work bound to the plastic rigidity of representation and kept our daydreams of liberation relegated to the long night of oppressing lucidity. Our only success was found in a share of guilt-free servitude and creature-comfort certainty. But this certainty was a commodity measured only in days and years, while the servitude was measured in something even less substantial. Our vacuum of unrequited release became filled with the detached apathy of tall tales and the false solidity of sweeping platitudes, while the trailing threat that we had been escaping from time immemorial remained nothing more than an innocuous abstraction of the mind: the villain in a fairy tale or the monster under your bed. But somewhere along the line we had forgotten that villains don't always stay confined to stories, that monsters are rarely found under beds, and that platitudes never fully take into account the actuality of human understanding.

I guess I was the first one who saw the handwriting on the wall—I was writing it after all. I was an idea man in all of this, one of the many designers. Ours were the tools of symbol and meaning. It was a simple function, and we took pride in its dignified humility. But the hubris of contrived humility persists for only so long as veiled pride has a way of revealing itself by denying responsibility for either side of any given outcome. We had insisted that we knew what we were doing but our efforts were always a shot in the dark, a matter of exuberant optimism and purposeful ignorance. It was the gamble of progress versus inevitability. But progress is progress, and an inevitability is an inevitability, and in matters of both luck and eternity, time and chance eventually manifest the other side of the spinning coin in one form or another. The side that we had bet against was coming up heads, the side that we had refused to acknowledge with the appropriate honesty to begin with, the side that was here long before any of us had started writing about saving grace or technological wherewithal.

Through the union of infinite chronological persistence and unbounded technological means, we had unwittingly crafted an abstract threat from our trailing past into an ingenious destruction in our coming future. A destruction that we now couldn't avoid as it was inherent in our course, and stopping was the one thing not built into this mechanism of now autonomous human history. This mechanism that had been crafted by everyone and no one out of a childish fantasy passed down from something called antiquity. This mechanism, the final liberty of which would be a total destruction, either in paced progress or in instant regress. It didn't matter—there were no two ways about it. It was enough to make the collective mind recoil into a state of denial, which it did; and the individual mind to flirt with break and dissolution in despair, and it had.

But even in despair, I found it noteworthy that particulars deviated within generalities; how the many differentiate from the singular while still maintaining inclusivity, and it is in this way that the individual mind, unlike the collective, wanders with remarkable intuition in its state of resignation. Spanning its own vast and aimless corridors with a playfulness that has no place in the world of straight lines and metallic consequences. I found a pleasure of release into this useless state of passivity where all things are permitted: meaningless shapes and movement, mechanical rules and distinctions, and the tender joys of basic human recognition—all things. And it was here also that I realized what had led to the purgatory of human history to begin with, what had undermined our externalized transcendence, and what our artificial intelligence had been missing all along—fate. A fate that had been negated by the mouth of emasculating recognition. A fate that had been superseded by the simultaneous extremes of humanity's dualistic sensibilities. A fate that, by all accounts found in the past or in the future, just did not exist.

And so my mind wanders in this place, uninhibited by maternal causality or binding paternal bookends, and I am reminded of an aphorism I had only previously half heard. I didn't understand it then, and I understand it less now, but it lifts my spirits in a way that contrived progress never could. And now, here, where humanity nears its end, here where our intelligence nears its limits, and here where the rock and the hard place are absolutely nothing but interchangeables, I guess we could all use a little levity—

"You can't have it both ways, but you can have it all three."

Life and Place

It was recognition that embraced the new little house as it stood proud at the break of its own dawn, proud above the hills of its own land, and proud beneath the light of the sun and other stars, and upon entry, the recognition was immediately reciprocated. It was true that he had built this house, but he never could quite admit as much to himself. He realized that the actual complexity of all things escaped his knowledge, including the dynamics of erecting walls and hammering nails, and it was this realization that had created a sense of gratitude even for the blessings of his own doing. And so he had built this house and this house had been given to him.

Throughout the years, he had marveled at the home's structural integrity and delighted in its unassuming endearments. He enjoyed the symmetry of every corner and every edge, while even the little imperfections, which had initially irritated him, had become emotionally integral over time. Every new day revealed fresh subtleties of the home's aesthetic value that he cherished with all the power of an unbridled sentimentality, a sentimentality that he considered justified through the broader implications of such affection.

As time passed, his mortality grew sharper in reflection. His sensibilities changed too, and his appreciation for the home followed suit in a slow shift from the sensual to something less apparent, something less defined but something ultimately more reliable: the empty space that the walls, floors, and roof revealed. He found that this space had a character all its own, a character that was manifested by the home's angles and hard surfaces; brought to life by his simple awareness. It was also the one element of the home that was not mirroring his own growing transience under the weight of passing time and shifting elements. For this reason, it became a permanently newfound joy and the perfect complement to a dignified deterioration. This space was where he really lived. This space was where the home had always returned his acknowledgement in its empty embrace.

But what is embrace without release? The little house was always his place to live, no one else's. This was apparent when he first entered in. But in the back of his mind, he knew it was also his place to die. It was love that had sealed this fate from the start. A love that was born of a bond that had never been joined and could therefore never be severed. It was this love that had shaped a proud and strong exterior, this love that had cared for an unassuming and gentle interior, and this love that had been present in the beginning and would be present in the end once more. As his conclusion drew near, he knew that this denouement would be one of complete abandonment, and so he made no arrangements for a new caretaker. His end was also to be the end of the little house as the movement of the world had already begun taking apart all that had been built little by little. And as dissolution met compliance, the vertical became horizontal, the up above met the down below, and everything in between deteriorated from the inside out until there was nothing left.

But to say that there was nothing left is only partially true, because this nothing left also happened to be his greatest joy. The empty space still remains. No longer recognizable, its characteristics formed by the various elements of physical structure are now gone, but the truth is that these were always precious but fleeting attributes anyway: particulars of an underlying unity. A unity that ultimately superseded the principles of both artificial construct and natural growth. The true depth of his personal totality had been revealed to him by a space defined by the hold of walls and other boundaries, but he knew that it was outside the confines of structure, shape, and distinction, at the end of an extensive and willing relegation, that the empty space, in release, would also realize its own totality, if just for a moment. Only to once more joyfully lose itself in the total embrace of all things: innumerable radiant stars, rolling grassy hills, and newly constructed little houses.

Red Herring

We were cleaning the dog pen and he wasn't saying a word. Wasn't much to talk about I guess. Manipulating dog shit doesn't lend itself to stimulating conversation. Come to think of it, he wasn't much of a talker to begin with. Nevertheless, I couldn't help but think that there was something else going on that day. It wasn't just the typical lack of communication. It was a focus in his eyes that held my curiosity. It was the look of being somewhere else entirely while maintaining a partial presence for the sake of responsibility or maybe company. I wondered where this somewhere else entirely was. I was sure of one thing; it wasn't in this damned dog pen. At least, I hoped it wasn't. I wanted to just come out and ask him what the hell was the matter, but I simply couldn't find it within myself. We just didn't have that kind of relationship. I found this unfortunate, especially when considering how much time we spent together. This was *our* job after all. It just seemed like we were always on different wavelengths. There never was that conscious moment of overlapping differences where understanding could be recognized and then felt in silent acknowledgment.

I would have liked a moment like that. A deeper connection between us, something more substantial than the ins and outs of our shared labor. But for a variety of reasons, I never could put this into words. An element of my own weakness I suppose.

I picked up the pace of my work as if sped up monotony could more effectively hold my attention; an effort to spite his emotional disconnect through a contrived disinterest. I wasn't having much luck. I just couldn't fathom what his problem could have been. It's not like he was the only one with problems. I was in here too. I found myself craving that warm feeling of knowing that follows a satisfactory explanation. And in the total absence of such an explanation and such a feeling, I began picturing a fictional narrative that could have preceded our shift. An expository list of occurrences leading up to this point that would logically define his apparent discontent—this was a regular habit of mine. But as I was finishing up a very elaborate and very plausible scenario in my mind's eye, a particular imaginary detail sparked a troubling realization. I now knew that whatever was bothering my coworker could have been anything, literally anything, anything and everything. I felt a slight dizziness as I teetered on the precipice of my own imagination. Stepping back, I thought that it would probably be better to, once again, pick up my pace and forget the whole thing. But, once again, I just couldn't; and the more I privately considered the internal situation of my coworker, the more I felt embarrassed. Embarrassed by my own internal rumination on the state of a person who was within earshot. I had to say something.

"Hey, you missed something on that side of the pen. It's back there a little ways. Did you just not see it?"

...

"That's all right, you'll get it on the way out."

...

"So, you got any plans after we get out of here?"

...

"I'll take that as a no. I don't either. Come to think of it, I hadn't even thought of it myself until just now. That's kind of weird, isn't it?"

...

"Oh, I forgot to ask, have you made any headway on, well ... you know?"

...

"Okay, okay, forget I mentioned it."

...

"Good lord, do you smell that? What am I saying? How

could you not. You know that smell is the one thing that I never get used to about this job. I swear that smell has become a part of my DNA. It just doesn't wash off no matter how hard I scrub. Did you ever notice that? How that smell just follows you everywhere you go?"

...

...

"Ummm...hey...you know, I'm not just talking to hear the sound of my own voice. You could indulge me with a response every now and then. Considering how much time we spend in here it would be nice if we could talk more candidly. I mean, not just the typical work banter, but talk about, I don't know, nothing in particular."

...

"Okay, well, I can't make you talk. You've got me beat there, congratulations. But you know something? You can't shut me up. Did you ever consider that? You can't shut me up. You're gonna have to listen to this. You're going to have to listen to anything and everything I have to say. And once I get going I just keep on going. I'm telling you I just keep on going. I'm going to go on talking and talking and talking and you're just gonna have to listen to every word of it. Are you good with that? I said, are you good with that!?"

...

"You really are a hard head, aren't you? Not much gets through that thick skull of yours, that's pretty clear. In fact, that's really the only thing I know about you for sure, and that's not saying much."

...

"You know who you remind me of?"

...

"You remind me of ... did you ever meet the owner of this place? You must have. When you started here you must have been introduced. Kind of a strange character. Wasn't much of a talker either. Which was why when he did talk it was all the more bizarre. What I mean by that is what he did say was usually odd and the oddity was amplified by his typically quiet nature. There was one thing in particular that he used to go on about whenever things got too sticky around here, as we both know they sometimes do. Anyway, it was the strangest thing you ever heard. The truth is, I never knew what the hell it meant but part of me liked hearing it. I mean, I thought the guy was out of his mind but it was still nice to have his words directed toward me, even if they didn't make sense. I guess now that I think about it, it was better that it didn't make sense. I don't know why. I guess I liked the ambiguity, but that didn't stop me from spending a lot of time trying to figure out what he was getting at—a lot of time. Anyway, maybe you can make heads or tails of it. It went like this, well, first of all, do you know what a red herring is?"

...

"A red herring is a kind of fish, but the term red herring in this story of his referred to a usage of this fish and not the fish itself. Anyway, in this sense, there are three red herring variations that you'll have to keep in mind.

"The first was a method of using the fish's pungent smell to train hunting dogs—actually, there are conflicting stories about this. Some say it was used to train horses, not dogs. I guess I'm not really sure which is true, but horses, dogs, or everything in between, the gist is that it was a method of training to seek toward a certain goal. That's all you really need to know. Far as I can tell, his story was more symbolic than anything. The finer specifics are more or less irrelevant.

"Anyway, the second usage would be a means of throwing off the trail of a would-be pursuer. You know, like if a convict is escaping and he uses the smell to throw off a pack of trailing hound dogs so as to avoid being caught in his pursuit of freedom. Kind of a weird idea, isn't it? Again, the particulars aren't really important, so don't get too hung up on them.

"The third is the most blatant usage, but strangely, for that reason it's also harder to explain so bear with me. To begin with ..."

It was at this moment that I realized that my coworker had left. Or rather, I assumed he'd left, as I didn't actually see him leave. I guess I was too damned interested in hearing the sound of my own voice to notice what was going on around me. I just really wanted to get that stupid story right. I was hoping to get his input on what he thought it might mean. I couldn't help but wonder how long I had been talking to myself. I felt kind of ridiculous about it, so much so that I could feel my face turning red in my own embarrassment. I sat down on a bag of Triple Crown for a few moments, unsure of a couple of things. First of all, I wondered why my coworker had just taken off like that. Why didn't he let me know he was leaving? Also, where did he go? We came in together, and, well ... we came in together.

I stayed and continued working it over a little longer before I decided I would leave too. This job of ours was too big for one person and I didn't see any end in sight. But as I was leaving, I remember thinking that maybe my coworker had gotten something from my clumsy attempt at communication after all. Maybe that was why he left. Maybe I said something that revealed an overlapping difference between us. The kind of thing that once recognized can only be acknowledged in silence anyway. It was a nice thought, and it made me feel better as I continued leaving. But then I started thinking that it would have been nice if he would have said *something* before he left. Something to let me know that I could stop talking, and enjoy the silence too, for crying out loud. And then it occurred to me that maybe for some reason he couldn't tell me where he was going and that's why he left so inconspicuously, because of course I would have wanted to know his destination. That made comforting sense to me on my way out. But what about my feelings, I thought. My whole stupid monologue had been an effort to express an empathy toward my coworker, an empathy that seemed blatantly unreciprocated with his utterly silent departure. But then I thought that even though he didn't say anything out loud, it was possible that he'd thought about saying something as he left. You know, a silent consideration. Something that he would have liked to have said to me but couldn't for the reasons previously noted. This pacified me momentarily but, then, while still leaving, I began wondering about the specifics. What exactly could he have thought about saying? What would have perfectly befit the situation? I decided, for some reason, among all else, that this was crucially important.

I began picturing a fictional narrative in my mind: my coworker leaving with my back turned while I continued talking, still self-engaged with whatever the hell I was going on about, and then I contemplated his parting courtesy. Maybe just a standard goodbye? No, that would have been too formal. Perhaps just a casual wave? No, something about that just didn't fit the narrative. Maybe something longer, more intricate and explanatory? But how long? How intricate? How explanatory? It was hard to say. I went on and on like this for a particular length of time before it finally hit me. It was so obvious that I almost missed it completely, but somehow it hit me. I knew exactly what his imaginary parting gesture would have been. It encompassed everything that I needed to feel a total certitude, it was everything necessary to quell my ceaseless questioning. It left no loose ends whatsoever. It was perfect. Or, almost perfect. There was one lingering problem, as there always seems to be. You see, this realization of mine came to me rather secretly and only in the silent recognition of its own absence after I myself was already gone and, for some reason, at that point, it no longer mattered.

Gomer

There is a moral. I would like to get that out of the way up front for the sake of empathy if nothing else. Because you see, personally, I've always disliked waiting to find out if there is intended wisdom within the confines of a story. In fact, if you catch me in a hyperbolic enough mood, I might even claim to hate such waiting. And I would be remiss if I subjected you to something I myself, under the right circumstances, had a hatred for. I will say though that this hatred is not the same type of hate that Gomer had for orange. That's right, Gomer, that's right, hate, and that's right, orange. Just plain old regular orange. If that strikes you as odd, you're not alone. Initially, I wasn't sure what to do with the knowledge of such an unusual characteristic myself.

Now, don't get me wrong, there isn't anything inherently wrong with a hatred of orange. Hatred is a natural part of life, as we all know, and orange is as good a thing to hate as any other, I suppose. The problem with Gomer's hatred was more an issue of action than an oddity of object. You see, Gomer was kind of stupid about things, and this stupidity reached some unfortunate limits when it came to the peculiar hatred at the heart of this story. Sure, there were lots of things that Gomer loved that could have balanced the tilt of his choices, but none of them could match the very love that he had for his particular hatred—so you can see the dilemma. Orange's very existence was enough to render all other joys in Gomer's life tainted and unfulfilling. So, Gomer did the only thing that seemed reasonable to him and his obtuse way of experiencing life. He decided, without much consideration and with some questionable counsel if I do say so myself, to dedicate himself to the hunt and eradication of orange. Yes, Gomer had chosen a purpose and he acted in coordination with this purpose with all of the subtlety of a vigilant village idiot.

Everywhere Gomer went, orange was a constant element of exacerbation. It taunted Gomer, obscuring a clear vision of his world as the ever-present fact of its most abhorrent flaw (according to Gomer that is). His travels took him to and fro as he worked for his goal with both diligence and compulsion. Pursuing the destruction of orange with an unconscious focus that allowed no room for much contemplation of anything else. Unfortunately for Gomer, orange turned out to be more elusive than could have been predicted. No matter how much progress Gomer seemed to make in one way or the other, he would once more realize the continuation of his nemesis somewhere out there in the distance; still haunting his world, still obstructing his life. It was imagination that kept Gomer on track. The imagination of the glorious victory he would one day taste. How his pursuit would finally end with the final and complete destruction of orange followed by the satisfaction he would feel when he reached his goal out there at the end of the line. But, in spite of conviction, a fool's a fool's a fool, and I guess that really is the moral of this story. As you have probably already guessed, old Gomer never did destroy orange. But it wasn't for a lack of trying. Just the opposite in fact, as one day, bless his heart, Gomer died in the fury of his own efforts, collapsing into a glorious pile of pride, certainty, and ignorance. I'll spare you the ugly details of Gomer's demise, but you probably have your own notion as to what those details spell out and, for the purposes of this story, that notion will do just fine.

The truth is that I'm going to miss Gomer, after all, he was a good-hearted fellow, heck, maybe that's the real moral of this story. While his actions were of the foolish variety, there was something about his sincerity that evoked within me a sense of empathy for the old boy. Plus, if I'm truly being honest with you, dear reader, I owe a lot to Gomer's folly. You see, I'm a simple man and I had a simple life. I had never known real prosperity before I was introduced to Gomer the donkey and his unshakable motive of resentment, a motive, I might add, that was quite contrary to Gomer's happier yet less productive counterparts. He really was a good-hearted fellow, that's worth repeating, but dammit, he never could figure out that old carrot on a string trick. There's no doubt that you can understand why I can't help but feel partially responsible for what happened to Gomer out there in those fields. But go easy on me, friend. The truth is that Gomer had made up his mind about orange long before he met me and, what can I say, times were tough. Plus, I never deny the silver lining on the other side of a tragedy, even if it's a fool's tragedy that I end up playing a small role in. And please forgive me if you sense within the spaces of this story a measure of questionable humor because, as a simple man, I never deny that either. But for my sins and in remembrance of Gomer, I won't bait you any longer toward the true moral of this tale, as I'm sure you've already spotted it out there in the distance. In fact, I'll bet by now you can even guess what it is that I farm. But in case you haven't quite figured it out, I'll give you a hint—it ain't oranges.

A Figure of Illustration

I had consistently been running late. Also consistent was the expectation of punctuality. I had to hurry to find him.

I had forgotten his name. This in itself was not a problem. What was a problem was the corresponding feeling: the aggravation of a memory that you can sense but is still somehow out of reach. I figured that once I saw him again the name would come back to me. The *him* in question was the figure in an old flip-book that had been given to me at some point in my youth. I guess it was ultimately boredom that had brought him to mind, but what had started as the passive musing of childhood recollection was becoming an adult test of personal willpower. I had to remember that name.

In case you aren't familiar, a flip-book is a cheap novelty of illusion, a collection of pages on which each sheet has the same image only slightly altered from one page to the next. When cycled through fast enough, these images coalesce and give the impression of a singular representation, a singular life. This particular flip-book, even by flip-book standards, was a simple one: a white background with nothing more than a repeating black figure. It was a boring contrivance to be sure, but beyond the boredom and beyond the contrivance, there was an uncanny quality to the way the figure, or the sum of these parts, moved, alone yet driven by the whims of another. As I would flip through the book, the little figure would dutifully and indeed selflessly meet my expectations, but I couldn't help but think, in some way, that there was in fact something in it for him. Something beyond the banality of blank white pages and choreographed movement; his own secret purpose. A promise beyond the last page. A page he would never go beyond. A promise he could never realize. I couldn't help but feel a childish compassion for the little figure. The kind of compassion that is almost too much for one person to take: the overwhelming engulfment of a love and empathy that simply cannot be acted upon.

After sifting through an endless minutiae of stored clutter, I found the flip-book in the darkness of an empty drawer. I contemplated how long the little figure had been there alone in the stillness of his own division. No one to make him move, no one to make him live. Meanwhile, the sun was beginning to set. As I opened the book, the light of dusk penetrated the room and revealed the disappearance of an expectation in a cascade of empty white pages. A breeze of momentum reached out from the book and gently enveloped me as each barren sheet appearing and disappearing left me with a peculiar feeling of alienation. When I reached the last page, I found myself transfixed with its emptiness; there was no way through that last page to the other side. The book was a linear course from beginning to end. That was all he had, it was all he was. The little figure's conclusion had always been on that last page, but now, somehow, he was not. I gave the last page one more look—there was no way through. Putting the book down, I noticed something else in the empty drawer, something I had somehow missed. It was bright and vivid, with a striking sense of depth. I didn't recognize it. No time to ponder, I was already out the door, running late.

My pace was brisk to the point of being forced. I was determined to arrive before the passing of time could render my destination irrelevant. There was conviction in my gait, sincerity in my heart, and a breeze at my back, which I interpreted as nothing less than a sign of my own certitude. I had a responsibility, and it was one I intended to honor. But in spite of the assurance of certitude or the drive of conviction, there was something else newly present in this amalgamation of variables that had found me diligently on my way. Something in the back of my mind, something I could no longer ignore: the little figure's name, still just out of reach. His curious absence from the flip-book had left me without a spark to illuminate the misplaced memory. I could almost feel the quality of the names pronunciation, could almost touch it. The task of recalling a forgotten name brought on by nostalgia was now a scramble for reassurance in the face of a disappearance, a disappearance that I was taking quite personally. If I could remember his name, I thought, those empty pages would at least tell a story. I would at least have a conceptual counterpoint to project meaning onto the void of an empty rolodex. The movement in my mind now paralleled the movement of my feet: a pressed internal search that drove my thoughts onward in unison with my body. The faster I moved through space the faster I moved through mind. All the while, the sidewalk stretched out before me. Each step I took implying its correlative at the other end, out there in the distance.

At this point it was dark and had been for some time. My footsteps echoed through the still, hollow air, while my mind oscillated between the forgotten name and a timely arrival. Both were eluding me. It was only in a casual glance beyond a retrograde limitation that a new elusion now commanded my attention—the night had silently overtaken the sidewalk. A chill of fear ran up my spine as I came to a startled halt. I stood motionless before a previously unimaginable uncertainty. My destination had always been so certain, so concrete that I hadn't even considered its specifics. This lack of details had always been inconsequential beneath the unwavering assurance of the sidewalk, but now, behind a blanket of black, the sidewalk could do me no more favors. I could no longer overlook what I was missing— I had no idea where I was going. I searched myself for a mental cue to bring a conceptual sensation to my destination, but there was a growing numbness that had started in my mind and was therefore already ahead of this curve. I looked around myself for a new way, a more promising direction that I might forget my freshly opened inadequacy, but I found that I was boxed in by the inky black of a starless night and all other directions merely confirmed this fact. Finally, in desperation, I went to call for help only to find that my vocal chords had gone catatonic and the rest of my muscles were following suit, and it was here, for the first time, that I slowly felt myself disappear into the darkness.

There is no way of knowing how long I was there. I felt nothing, including the sense of passing time. Strangely enough, this feeling of nothing was not initially apparent to me, not even when contrasted with any one of the multiplicity of actualized moments the course of a life presents to a person upon reflection. No, this nothing I felt came to my attention only through the emergence of a particular sound. It was a familiar sound but a sound I could not put my finger on no matter how hard I tried. This sound came in the silence of the night as the breeze at my back once again revealed itself to me as the directive of certitude, but now I didn't move, I couldn't move ... I wouldn't move. The push of air contrasting with my own stillness released a rush of energy from somewhere within that jolted my body and ignited a fire in my voice as I cried out through the darkness. This cry was the incoherent upheaval of everything untouchable inside of me. It was something that was too much to take, something that simply could not be acted upon. It meant nothing and referred to no one—it was the name of the little figure. How could I have forgotten?

I felt an ease of clarity come over me and, just like that, my destination became obvious—a sigh of relief; by now, the sun was beginning to crest the horizon and its light illuminated the way. The sidewalk once again stretched endlessly into the distance while I found myself standing directly in the center of one of its four-cornered slabs. As the sidewalk continued on, I found a particular fascination in how still my own feet were. I couldn't help but think of that last empty page. No way through indeed.

A gentle breeze played with the leaves of a nearby tree as I strolled off of the sidewalk and rested my back against the tree's trunk. The grass was cool and the tree was easy. It was the perfect spot to enjoy the break of dawn. The sun made its ascent into an empty sky and I watched as an ocean of color spilled out across the horizon. The light danced with the endless variations of empty space as my new day came to life in a brilliant living collage of diaphanous shapes and distinctions, hues and gradations. And it was here that I disappeared once again, only this time in plain view, only this time behind the light, only this time before the sun.

I was right on time.

***

The *sui generis* nature of the universe leaves something to be desired at the heart of humanity, a void that is reflected in the ever-expanding breadth of existence, a single interval without measure. Where is responsibility in eternity? For the question there is no answer, only a vision. The vision ascends from the sound of the infant's cry. The vision descends into the silence of the tree's passivity. And the vision is veiled by the inexhaustible ramblings of mutual irresponsibility.

Blind Singularity: A Dialogue

Part 1

Number 1- Sir, have you seen the news?

— Of course I've seen the news, Number 1! How effective could I possibly be if I hadn't seen, above all else, the Goddamn news … what have you heard?

Number 1- Well, apparently, there was a bombing yesterday, sir.

— Son of a bitch! Where's ground zero?

Number 1- Well, I'm afraid at this point it's hard to say, sir.

— What do you mean it's hard to say? How hard is it to give an exact location, Number 1?

Number 1- We're checking into it, sir. As soon as I know, you'll know.

— No shit, Number 1! That goes without saying! Don't state the obvious, it makes you sound ridiculous and is a waste of precious time!

Number 1- Yes, sir.

— How are things on the front as of now?

Number 1- Quiet, sir.

— The calm before the storm.

Number 1- Sir?

— What, do you think this was an isolated incident, Number 1? Is there such a thing? I mean, have you ever in your life seen such a thing, Number 1!?

Number 1- Well sir, I suppose that …

— That was a rhetorical question, Number 1. A little slow on the uptake aren't you? There *will* be more attacks. You can mark my word on that.

Number 1- What do you suggest, sir?

— We have to hit them hard and we have to hit them fast.

Number 1- Who, sir?

— Dammit, Number 1! How dense is that skull of yours? You know, sometimes I wonder if you and I are even in the same room when we're talking! Who do you think?

Number 1- The enemy, sir?

— You're damn right the enemy!

Number 1- Yes, sir.

— It's important that strength is recognized so we can get a handle on this thing. We need to hit them where it hurts so they can see plain as day that we mean business.

Number 1- Sir?

— Answering arms with arms, Number 1!

Number 1- Yes, sir, I gathered as much, but it seems to me that there may be other considerations at this point to, well ... consider.

— For example?

Number 1- Well, there is still the question of ground

zero, sir. I think that should be addressed first and foremost, wouldn't you agree?

— No, I would not agree Number 1. And I would appreciate it if you wouldn't make assumptions without knowing for damn sure they are the correct ones!

Number 1- Correct ones?

— The stakes are too high for you to be throwing unverified opinions around with such reckless abandon, Number 1!

Number 1- Yes, sir.

— Anything else?

Number 1- Well, what about motive, sir?

— Motive?

Number 1- Yes, sir.

— Number 1, I'm not sure there is anything more clearly defined at this point than motive.

Number 1- Sir?

— What are we talking about Number 1?! The motive is perfectly self-evident, and if you give me one more "sir?" before you order a strike, it's gonna be your ass! I can't stand that inflection in your voice, especially after an order.

Number 1- Inflection, sir?

— Yes, just like that! Now, don't get cute, Number 1!

Number 1- Yes, sir.

— I want retaliation and I want it yesterday, do you understand me!?

Number 1- Yes, sir.

— Good. Now, report back when at all appropriate, Number 1.

Part 2

— What's the news, Number 1?

Number 1- There has been a bombing, sir.

— I should certainly hope so. This is a war after all, Number 1. Don't want to be caught with our pants down when the lights go out, do we? Now, where did we strike?

Number 1- Well, it's difficult to say, sir.

— Come again, Number 1?

Number 1- We're checking into it, sir, and as soon as I know I'll ... well ... we're checking into it.

— Didn't you receive your orders, Number 1?

Number 1- Yes, sir.

— Well, what's the problem?

Number 1- Well, I suppose the problem is a matter of precision, sir.

— Precision? Number 1, this is a war, not brain surgery.

Number 1- Yes sir, but I'm afraid the characteristics of the enemy aren't totally understood at this point, sir, which makes it difficult to know where exactly to strike.

— But we already struck.

Number 1- That's true, sir.

— I'm not sure how those two facts compute, Number 1.

Number 1- It is kind of a mystery sir, and again, we're looking into it.

— A mystery? We're looking into it?

Number 1- Yes, sir.

— How did you get this position, Number 1? Who in their right mind had the audacity to give you that title of yours?

Number 1- Well, sir, it isn't exactly ...

— Rhetorical, Number 1!

Number 1- Yes, sir.

— Now, what do you mean it's difficult to say? What do you mean we're looking into it? Who precisely did we hit?

Number 1- The enemy, sir?

— Is that a question number 1? Because that sounded like a question. I would hope at this point in the game one or two things would be understood on your part. And when I ask you a question, you can damn well assume I don't want another question in return. Is that asking too much, Number 1?

Number 1- Yes, sir ... I mean, no, sir.

— So, who did we hit?

Number 1- The enemy, sir.

— That's better. Now, how are things on the front?

Number 1- Quiet, sir.

— Son of a bitch.

Number 1- Sir?

— Number 1, I certainly hope I don't have to explain the whole calm before the storm thing to you again.

Number 1- No, sir, but do you think it applies in this situation?

— How do you mean?

Number 1- I think it's possible that relativity comes into play here, sir.

— Number one, I think we have all we need from the likes of Einstein at this point, thank you very much, and to be honest with you, I don't think even he could fully appreciate the gravity of what we're dealing with here. Now, hit 'em again.

Number 1- But sir ...

— For Christ's sake, Number 1, don't you want peace?

Number 1- Of course, sir. Don't we all? I mean, I think we all do, sir.

— Well dammit, Number 1, do you think we're gonna have peace by just sitting around here doing nothing? We're in an ordeal here. It's true, we didn't ask for this, but by God we are going to finish it. Now enough with the stalling, I want preemptive action, Number 1, and I'm not going to wait until tomorrow to get it! Do you understand me!?

Number 1-

— Number 1??

Number 1, I need you to listen closely to me because I don't want to have to keep repeating myself. I've had it about up to here with your lack of insight into the nature of our war. I don't have the time or the energy to spell every little thing out for you. And I'm afraid if you don't get your head in the game soon, you're going to be stripped of your title when this thing is all over; do you understand me?!?

Fundamental Paradox
―――∽―――

The finger was there from the start. What I mean is that I didn't actually witness its entry up and through the surface of the floor on which I now stood. The event that had apparently preceded the stillness of what I saw before me had somehow gone completely unnoticed.

It seemed to be around twelve feet wide. That is a rough estimate, but a good one. The tip of the protruding finger and the matching hole of its entry point were at least twice as wide as the average man is tall. I remember this because, on first inspection, I didn't even consider the dimensions of what I was observing. It was only after a brief and then doubled glance downward that the scope of things, contrasted with my previous indifference, immediately became of the utmost importance. In my left hand, I held a black cube about half the size of a standard shoebox. The other hand held nothing. Nothing but a fist with one finger rebelling into an elongated point towards and through the top of the mysterious object in my hand.

As the oddity of my circumstances began to reverberate with consciousness, I reflexively removed my finger while simultaneously dropping the cube to the floor. Looking up again, the giant hole in the floor before me now laid empty. I suddenly felt something from above on the top of my head, a breeze perhaps. The kind of breeze that signifies an opening. This was particularly strange because there was no wind and no hole in sight other than the one before me. After considering this lack of movement in the air and my peculiar and contrary sensory response, my attention was drawn back to the hole, the floor, the cube, and to my own strange relationship to the three. The cube laid on its side a few feet from where I had dropped it, about halfway between myself and the gaping floor opening. Reluctantly, I approached the cube just behind the rate that my initial shock was evolving into a hesitant curiosity. Picking the cube up off of the floor revealed a weight that I hadn't noticed while holding it moments before. The cube was smooth to the touch with sharp angles and, as far as I could tell, perfect symmetry. It had a light sheen but not to the point of being reflective. After studying its surface, I took notice of the small hole my finger had previously occupied. I held the cube up to my eye and looked through this opening. Nothing but one strange color. The same color that seemed to envelop whatever space it was that I now occupied. (more on that later.) After a few moments of reservation, I again poked my finger through the hole in the cube. And again, before me now was the immense appendage doppelgänger. One by one, I replaced each previous finger with the next, each corresponding from the floor with its king-sized equivalent.

Upon removing the last of my probing digits from the cube, the hole in the floor once more laid void. I set the cube down gently. After quelling a paralyzing measure of trepidation, I made my way up to the gigantic hole in the floor for further inspection. I was only a couple of feet away when I began to see the absence of space just beyond the raised rim of the giant finger's entry point, an absence represented by nothing but black. It was a deep black so striking that it seemed to have its own consistency. Reaching out to test my vision revealed not consistency but potency as my hand up to the wrist disappeared in the darkness of the hole right before my eyes. Thinking of the giant finger now, I glanced back at the cube on the floor, only to realize that the side of the cube with the tiny hole was facing away from me and out of sight. Moving with conviction, I retrieved the cube and brought it to the edge of the hole in the floor. It was at this point that I caught hold of myself in a pause. A pause in which I attempted to slow an expanding understanding that was rushing over me like a dark, swift water, threatening to consume me in an unnervingly apathetic course of flow. After a moment taken to absorb the total lack of reassurances or certainties my situation afforded me, I again reached into the darkness of the hole in the floor. As my hand disappeared before me, it immediately and quite matter-of-factly reappeared to the scale that I had suspected, that I had feared, from the tiny hole in the black cube.

At this point, my behavior became sporadic, derivative, and difficult to recount. I found myself locked into a strange emotional amalgamation of curiosity and claustrophobia as I toiled compulsively in an effort to cope with the perplexity of my situation. I'll spare you the details of my actions with the exception of two cogent notes worth mentioning. The first in the form of an image: a person standing at the edge of a giant black cube, contemplating suicide. The second in the form of an analogy: the exhibition of a descending and potentially endless video feedback loop. Everything in between I'll leave to your imagination.

Before I go further, I suppose a little more about my whereabouts are in order. Upon my initial considerations, I couldn't make out much of where I was. The reason for this was difficult to describe, but for the sake of brevity, just imagine, and this will take some imagining, an opaque luminosity that would best be summed up as the color of silence. It was a color that permeated this place and was no more clearly represented than in its embodiment of the indeterminably sized surface on which I now stood, the surface that had no point of contrast other than the giant hole in the floor, myself, and the black cube. This color, this expanse of visual monotony, rendered me myopic in my observations, and it wasn't until after my externalized inquisition into the nature of the box and the two holes that I began to form some semblance of a notion as to what type of structure I occupied. But I couldn't be sure.

I couldn't be sure—I guess that's initially why I started walking. Walking away from the giant hole, away from the cube, and away from my unfathomable predicament. But, as is so often the case in these matters, I carried my predicament along with me even though my hands hung freely at my sides clutching nothing but themselves. Part of this walk, a small part, was in fact an effort to confirm my suspicions as to the nature of my whereabouts, searching for a wall somewhere in the distance, somewhere unknown, a flat solid surface that would correspond with the external symmetry of the little black cube; a flat solid surface that would correspond with my expectations. But, expectations aside, what I really wanted from this hypothetical wall was an end, an end represented by a surface onto which I could project an assertion of the absurdity of my situation and then leave it. Leave it for some other poor sap to find. I thought he or she would possibly get something good out of it, something that I lacked the perspective to see for myself. But there was no such wall at the end of my journey and no such sap to speak of. What there was was a return. A return to the start. A return to the hole. A return to the cube. "Full circle" has never been so apt a description.

I sat down between the cube and the hole, collapsing into my own exhaustion as I began to wonder for the first time, really wonder, how I had arrived at this place. My memory traveled back only so far before being obliterated by a giant finger sitting motionless in a corresponding giant hole. Whatever had come before that was gone. Gone, gone. I thought about it and thought about it and thought about it until finally I realized something in the circular movement of my own contemplation: I wasn't thinking about it at all any more. I wasn't thinking about anything. My mind was a blank space and in its void was this place in which I found myself: the hole, the cube, the floor and its spherical nature, and above all, the color of silence and the black. That was all there was.

I could no longer mask my own knowledge with the self-induced confusion cultivated by a potentially endless array of fool's errands. I knew that part of me had been stalling this entire time. This whole thing: this place, the hole, the cube, the totality of my predicament, was all some kind of postponement, a postponement for a transference that I could just barely sense but that I had sensed all along. It was the kind of sense that was just vague enough that it could have either been a reverberation from the past or an anticipation of the future and it was this kind of uncertainty, coupled with my own distrust, that had found me here. It was obvious to me how to leave this place, and no matter how vehemently I tried to convince myself otherwise, deep down, it always had been. The foundation of my quandary was simply the upholding of a here and a there. This wasn't so much an unfathomable confinement as it was a superficial refuge. A safety blanket. My previous experimentation with the hole and the cube had been absent of one obvious exploit: I knew that If I stepped through the hole in the floor with the cube in tow, bringing all aforementioned elements to one point of unified reference, I would leave this place, I would no longer be held to it, and I would see the other side of Fundamental Paradox.

Let's suppose that I took this step, if only for the sake of this story. How could I describe the result of such a passage? How could I describe the freedom such a passage would precede? How could I describe my entrance out of Fundamental Paradox? Well, before I go any further, I must confess that the box and the floor and the hole never actually existed, at least not in any real sense of the word. But, in order to present a paradox, there must be some definitive limitations to introduce the point, and the floor, the hole, and the cube as artifacts were as appropriate a list of limitations as any other. But what of the aforementioned departure? What of the inspiration for this story and the end product of my elucidation? How can I describe the reality on the other side of a hole that did not exist? How can I describe a place beyond paradox that fundamentally knows no limitations and is boundless through and through? Well, the most important detail of the place on the other end of this story was my own absence from it. I was never there, and I will repeat that, I was never there. I never saw it, I never felt it, I never experienced it—yet I know it well. How could this be, you might ask? The only answer that I can give to you is that this place on the other side held nothing whatsoever, and this nothing whatsoever naturally excluded myself. But you must understand that when I say nothing whatsoever, what I mean is a special kind of everything. The kind of everything that tends to lose grounds of credibility when logic comes into play. So how can it be expressed? How can it be described? How can it possibly be represented?

What of its shape, you might ask? There was no shape. How could there be any particular shape among an infinite variation of figures constituting an undifferentiated whole? Not so much as the straight of an edge or the curl of a line.

What of its color, you might wonder? There was no color. How could there be any particular color among a spectrum of innumerable unified hues? Not so much as the black of a cube or the color of silence.

What of its movement?

What of its movement?

There was movement.

Somehow, among the infinite paces and directional avenues of this place, something uniformly stood out.

Something was noted.

It was a simple pace repeating itself at various lengths.

A descending rhythm of two relational directions.

Repeating over and over again.

From one direction to the other.

From one direction to the other.

And it was only after the movement stopped and stillness was affirmed that the nature of the reality on the other side of Fundamental Paradox was revealed. Because the moment the movement stopped—the very moment—I was free to see that, in spite of logic, reason, or certain assertions projected onto a flat solid surface somewhere unknown ...

I was there after all.

The Empty Theater

It is still here after the lights have all dimmed and the crowds have all left, here in the stillness of absence and the silence between echoes. It is forgotten in the fulfillment of entertainment, and it is abandoned in the completion of performance, but it is still here. Its emptiness holds steady in the darkness of dormancy, and its energy goes unmoved in the singularity of one-sided potential.

And then the curtain lifts.

An act flows with conviction through the spaces of its script. In the corridors of mind, the procession of scene and dialogue guides intent. Memory serves well as lines are at the will of command, and marks are of second nature to momentum. A focus sharpens and the performance reaches a new level of representation. There is now a solidity to this act: a rigidity that has materialized out of the basic elements of theater, formed by passion, execution, and commitment. This solidity is refined to sharp edges and opaque form that first define only to then blur once again—an audience appears and then fades into an impersonal amalgam of disunited perspectives, performances emerge and then vanish behind the growing shadow of cultivated self-involvement, and the actor asserts and then dissolves into the embodiment of his own abandonment, lost without trace in the timeless pursuit of the role of a lifetime.

In this guided spontaneity of craft, the performer is forgotten to himself as he is now subjected to a story that he no longer knows, a story that he no longer controls. Where the actor had found reference in the placement of set, *he* now finds confusion in the boundary of structure. Where the actor had found levity in the support of the stage, *he* now finds gravity in the contention of an unmoving ground. This stage is now a hostility, and this set an alienation, and in the blinding light of his own performance, he finds himself estranged. Estranged from the theater, estranged from himself.

A softness melts within him to contrast the density of his external opposition and the assertion of his act recedes into the dimension of feelings unseen. But here he is met with an invisible opposition, the opposition of expectation; an expectation that renders his movement hollow and contrived in the defensive maneuvering of a self-imposed critique. His body tightens and the wild depths of his emotional aptitude ignite in response to the trembling recoil of a directionless incentive—there is an escape drawing near, an escape behind the veiling curtains of an unplanned intermission, an intermission that he does not understand, an intermission that he cannot name, but an intermission that he now craves, that he now wills, as he moves toward the back of the stage, toward the shadows, and away from himself.

But as he steps back into the stillness of the darkness, the vitality of the stage light shines new. He can now clearly see the interdependent movement of the other performances before him, a movement he had not fully considered, a movement he had not fully understood. And as the intermission draws nearer, threatening to envelop not only his place in this act but the totality of the act itself, something inside of him gives way first, something he now sees in the requiting gaze of his beloved costars, something he now feels at a place that no longer has an outlier: a center that he cannot locate, a center that he cannot define, a center that is unquestionably his own. In the eyes of his costars, it is the wink of a shared secret, the implicit recognition of an unspeakable understanding, the subtle assurance of a truth that could never, ever be reproduced.

Pulling his focus down and away from the act before him, his eyes follow the floorboards as they reach toward the back of the stage, back toward his point of departure, and back toward a redemption beyond opposition. His gaze stops without hesitation, without presupposition, precisely where the illumination of the stage meets the darkness of his resignation. It is here that his fourth wall of critical discernment shatters not by his efforts, not by his concessions, but of its own volition, of its own recognition, falling effortlessly into hundreds of crystalline fragments beyond the artificial boundary of the stage at hand. Each piece freely coming to a receptive rest, giving subjective credibility to the unknowable objectivity of the empty theater: unique jewels through which the total performance is reflected within the collective imagination of independent perspectives. And with an authority that is both independently received and inclusively given, he steps out of the shadow of a private curtain fall, a true character enraptured into the universal witness of his opening night lights, now loosed of the arbitrary limitations of script and convention, the intermission is abandoned as this show must go on!

This is the actor's pinnacle, a pinnacle that is found in the remembrance of himself *within* the forgetfulness of his act. Here, his skill culminates in the impeccable balance of a total loss and a total gain: the visceral consciousness of a finite story and its infinite potential. It is the internalized triumph of the theater and it gives life to all external apotheoses. It is inherent in the fruition of romance's true love, in the explosion of comedy's deepest belly laugh, and in the exaltation of drama's ultimate victory.

But for the actor who acts in earnest through and through, for the actor whose story goes unacknowledged into the apathy of an unbounded intermission, and for the actor whose performance is lost within the unheard echo of an empty theater—it is known only as the melancholy of tragedy's bitter end …

Until the curtain lifts again.

How to Enter Heaven

"It is easier for a camel to pass through the eye of a needle than for a rich man to enter the kingdom of heaven."

What a curious notion, this comment about the impact of wealth on a particular person's fundamental well-being. The statement invariably conjures up images of physical contortion that hardly leave room for a living mammal on the other end of the process—much less a living mammal in paradise. Moreover, one can hardly fathom heaven's apparently minuscule point of entry for the rich man and the necessary feat that would surpass in difficulty the plight of our even-toed ungulate. But this comment about a particular man leads me to wonder about the general: the universal person beyond the ultimately trivial aspects of one's superficial stature. How does *anyone* enter into the kingdom of heaven? I find the answers that are readily available to be muddled in rehashed concepts and tired dogma, answers that without fail lead only to more questions upon further inspection, and answers that over the course of my life I've heard more times than I've bothered to count. Perhaps you have, too.

It seems that in order to produce any semblance of an answer to this question, one must first have some idea as to what heaven would actually be like for oneself, and it is here that I am drawn back to the particular. Like the rich man considering his wealth, one must consider their own heart of hearts when it comes to the question of a personal eternity. What would I want heaven to be? But it is here that my imagination is implored to do the impossible as I am overcome by a sea of never-ending abstractions: an endless list of ideals and expectations constituting a mere dream of perfection.

And so I dream.

I dream of a heaven beyond description. Where labels vanish into the sounds of their original nature. Where what you see can't be real, can't be brought to the level of intellectual acceptance that we call knowledge, yet what you see also can't be held down, can't be subdued beneath reality's visceral and uncompromising threshold.

I dream of a heaven where the past and the future exist simultaneously. Where hoped for potentialities presently mingle with the fertile wisdom of memory, forever culminating in the perpetual flowering of an unmoving transformation of creative expression.

I dream of a heaven where others aren't just others, but are all parts of oneself. Where, for you, they are them and for them you are you. Equal manifestations of an inward truth revealing the wonder of company and kinship that holds a depth of union that reaches to the ultimate limits only to pass effortlessly beyond.

I dream of a heaven where choices are made not through the redundant and distorting prism of rigid valuations but through the ever-present wisdom of the senses and the careful consideration of reciprocal response. Here, you have no enemies, only friends that have forgotten bonds, and where you recognize these friends not through the contrast of the adversarial but through the contrast of the absence from where these friends have come.

I dream of a heaven where there is no end and there is no beginning, and for that reason alone, beginnings and endings flourish. Comings and goings, exuberance and rest. Where you are here until you are not, and where you are not until you are here, and the void in between comings, this apparent interval of nothing, is actually you—precisely you.

And finally, I dream of a heaven where a dream in question could be nothing more than another dream's dream, and thus there is no necessity for doubt. Where any dream can be given truth through choice and cultivation, stimulating a seamless shift from the diaphanous to the opaque, something from nothing through the final acceptance of all encompassing transience. And it would be here, at this shift in sleep, that a dream would respond with a shift all its own, beginning anew as life at this place where you would open your eyes again and again and again, forever.

But the question still remains: what of an entry?

I can't help but think that one's admittance to this place of boundless inclusion could be nothing more than a benign notion stemming from a conceptual point of departure, a fleeting but necessary distinction from the overwhelming bliss and transcendent totality that such a place would encompass. From this standpoint, it is clear how one would "enter" heaven if it did in fact exist. Like the example of the camel, entry would indeed be predicated on the impossibly insubstantial but, unlike the example of the rich man, the difficulty of entering heaven would not hinge on the grip *to* one's wealth but would rather hinge on the grip *of* the proceeding: the awakening startle of a benevolent deception—the initial implication that you weren't already there.

To Divvy up a Stalemate

There are any number of things about God that people don't realize. One such peculiarity is that he never could quite decide whether or not he existed ... something to do with transcending duality. Nevertheless, the question intrigued him and after much deliberation that ultimately led nowhere, he decided to outsource the question to a couple of unwitting human debaters: the theist and the atheist. He would listen in on their exchange in the hopes of once and for all deciding whether he was or was not.

It just so happened that two such characters had recently entered into such a discourse with a friendly wager attached for good measure. The wager went as follows: if the theist could provide the strongest argument for his respective position, the atheist agreed that he would proclaim God's existence. This would of course be unbecoming of an atheist, and the idea of such a concession made him a bit nauseous, but he decided that the bet was worth the risk in a humanist effort to promote universal agreeability. On the other hand, if the atheist asserted his respective position with the soundest argument, the theist agreed that he would drink a pint of the atheist's favorite beer. This in turn would be unbecoming of this particular theist, and the idea of such a concession likewise made him a bit nauseous, but he decided that the bet was worth the risk in a religious effort to bring the true realization of God to humanity.

Now, the theist was clever. He knew that the atheist had already made up his mind on this matter, and that the only way to have a fighting chance in this type of contest was to turn the atheist's reasoning against him. Only then could the atheist see through his own conceptual folly.

"So you don't believe in God," said the theist. "The idea of an all-powerful creator seems silly to you in the light of your knowledge. You believe that the universe is a chaotic and random event that human beings have just happened to emerge out of. You fundamentally believe that the universe has no meaning and that it is all at the whim of chance, nothing more and nothing less. Would you say that this is true?"

"Yes," said the atheist.

"Then I ask you: if the universe is meaningless, wouldn't that also mean that your very assertion against God's existence, an assertion that is an aspect of the universe, would ultimately and likewise hold no meaning? And that by default, your argument would have no validity based on your own proposition?"

"..."

"If you agree with this reasoning, which I'll take from your silence that you do, you had better forget convincing *me* that God does not exist; the more pertinent question is, how are you going to convince *yourself*?"

God was impressed and took note.

Now, the atheist realized a potential checkmate when he saw one, but he had been in this type of contest before, and he knew that the only way to salvage a comeback win would be to turn the theist's reasoning against him. Only then could the theist see through his own conceptual folly.

"So you believe in God," said the atheist. "You believe in an all-powerful being who can do all things. You believe that this being created the heavens and the earth and that the meaning of your existence is fundamentally dependent on the dichotomy of creator and created. Would you say that this is true?"

"Yes," said the theist.

"Well, if God is all-powerful, and can do all things, is it not possible that he could become a human being himself? That he could impose all manner of limitations on his power, including the knowledge of his own

Godhood, and that he could roam the earth completely unaware of his true identity?"

"..."

"If you agree with this reasoning, which I'll take from your silence that you do, you had better forget convincing me that God exists; the more pertinent question is, how are you going to convince *yourself* that *you* are not him?"

God was impressed and took note.

It was here that the two debaters found themselves in an awkward position. Each party had contributed to the discourse in such a way that awarding a winner seemed totally arbitrary and merely a matter of taste. And, with no indifferent third party in sight to give a definitive judgment, the two fell silent.

Meanwhile, God also saw that both arguments had a validity that he could not quite deny, a revelation that, in spite of his own indecision on the matter, he was not expecting from the debaters and therefore a revelation that left him completely nonplussed. This was unbecoming of God and, in such a state, he couldn't help but feel a bit nauseous.

But, after all was said and done and the nausea had dissipated a bit, God decided to proclaim himself so, if for no other reason than the sake of agreeability, for he realized that in a fundamentally meaningless universe, even the most brazen of assertions were void of real truth anyway. And, as he set down the empty beer mug, he also realized that sometimes a cold and refreshing punishment can prove to be a pretty nice consolation prize.

A Certain Ambiguity

What was it that woke me? I suppose it may have been the wind. I thought I had heard it softly blowing somewhere in a dream. Or maybe it was the whir of my ceiling fan as it spun effortlessly above my bed. Or perhaps it was the sound of an over-fasted yearning typical of these kinds of mornings. I couldn't be sure. I don't know why it mattered to me but it did. I laid still, sinking ever deeper into the softness of my bed, listening for whatever was responsible for my eyes now being open in the darkness. For some reason, I needed to know the answer to this question. Maybe it was just my way of easing into the new day.

Maybe it wasn't that at all.

In my youth, mornings had been brought to life by my mother. Even now, I can see her quite clearly through the passivity of memory. She always wore a blue plush bathrobe over her plaid pajama pants and oversized white T-shirt. Her silver hair would be pulled back in a black hairband and her tortoise shell glasses would be resting low enough on her bridge that she could look over the rims to emphasize the empathy in her fresh morning eyes; an empathy that was already an overstated regularity. She would quietly enter my childhood bedroom just as the sun began to stream through the window, flowing like water to the empty spaces created by ill-fitting curtains and pouring warmth into the cool darkness of my nocturnal sanctuary. Gently resting her hand on my shoulder, she would allow the force of gravity to do most of the morning's dirty work. The dirty work being nothing less than the imposition of the entire world. The brief condemnation of a child to the pain of transition and the paradoxical syncope of an implicit ideal vanishing in self-distinction. My day-to-day salvation was found in two requiting hazel reflections and the respite of boundless maternal understanding: the woman at the edge of my bed patiently waiting for me.

This was how my childhood days would start, and it made sense, or at least sense enough. But my mother's mornings were now her own. And for me, there were no more quiet entries, no more gentle touches, and no more recognizing eyes to pull me safely into the birth of a new day.

As I contemplated the now-mute something that had rendered me conscious, I began to notice a multitude of audible nothings gently sounding off all around the room. When I say nothings, what I mean is that they were the type of particulars that are hardly even worth mentioning on their own merits, but, contrasted with whatever it was that woke me, they coalesced into a delicate unity of character and personality. And so I had company, strange company, but company nonetheless. This fellowship of sounding and hearing was broken by a movement from somewhere on the other side of my bedroom door. I now noticed only the silence. I stared up through the darkness at the black place where, on good faith, I knew my ceiling hung. I then looked toward the clock on the wall—as black as the ceiling. Irrespective of the time, I had not planned on being up this early, but I was awake and I couldn't undo that fact. So, reluctantly, I fell out of the dark warmth of my bedding and made my way toward the thin strip of light from the other room and out.

As I opened my bedroom door, the white morning light smacked me in the face, momentarily stifling my momentum. Pressing forward down the hallway, the dark western hickory creaked beneath me, shaking my overly rested eardrums, while the balls of my feet ached with every barefoot thud against the unwavering hardwood floor. Reaching the end of two towering parallel walls and their two-way directive, I was met with rigid granite countertops, oversized wood paneling, and the metallic sheen of heavily manufactured appliances. And it was here that I knew something was wrong; it was his silence that gave it away. I stood anxiously, pretending to wait for him to acknowledge me first. After an obligatory moment of deference, I blurted something. I can't remember what.

He snapped his focus to me in a way that would have made Newton proud. I could tell that he was disgusted by my lack of tact. His greeting was as hollow as the ache of my morning stomach—I had hoped for something different. I knew that he wanted me to come sit with him, but before I could oblige, he started to speak.

Tell me, son, he said, the quality of his voice teetering somewhere between embarrassment and pride, *what do you think?*

My mind began spinning as it fielded an endless barrage of possibilities: innumerable articles of minutiae. I had the strange intimation that I would search myself indefinitely before I found something worthwhile to say, something that he would have liked. I was about to pop. As if sensing this, he gave me another look, this one different than the first.

About art, he said correctively. *What do you think about art?*

I was immediately taken aback. My father had never so much as mentioned art before, much less engaged me in a formal conversation on the matter. But while this was a particularly odd subject to bring up apropos of nothing, what I found even more peculiar at that moment was the state of the walls in the house surrounding our encounter. This was obviously not the question he wanted to ask.

"I don't know."

My voice shook with a residual anxiety that had been trailing from moments before, catching up with me at the worst possible moment.

I didn't think so, he said.

As if compelling a response, he stared at me with a pause of implication. I awkwardly went to blurt again; mercifully, he cut me off.

You see son, it's important to know that art can, in fact, be misinterpreted, a mistake that typically stems from the wrong vantage point. The trouble is that there is a prevalent insistence to the contrary. An insistence that is empowered by a staggering number of intellectual conventions. This is a common misconception, so it's one worth prefacing with.

Some part of myself shifted.

The reason for this is that the true understanding of art always starts in a place that no one will ever see. It starts back in the depth of the place where all art begins. Now, this is no measured depth, no static state of absence. This depth is an inward recession, a movement in and of itself. And as this depth falls into its own falling, an expression conversely expands out in all directions, manifesting slowly at first only to increase in velocity exponentially; complexities within complexities all working together through nothing more than the vaguest of intent.

I shifted again. I couldn't get comfortable.

As this expression grows out toward its ultimate limits, the depth recedes toward its own point of demarcation. A certain type of end is drawing near and an uncertainty begins to be realized within and without. It is here that the artistic vision threatens to be lost without ever being witnessed firsthand ... this is a possibility.

His tone sharpened, and my attention met its edge.

But—all the while—secretly, there has been a single point of stillness hidden within all of this. Simple and understated, it goes unnoticed. And as this process of dual movements finally culminates as and then recedes into an impossible complexity, sometimes, somehow, this single point of stillness remains to rise in its place of resignation. This, son, is the place where the true revelation of the artistic masterpiece can be experienced as it was intended.

My father's talking subsided but his explanation continued on. I couldn't imagine what would warrant such a grandiose soliloquy. I was terrified of knowing what it was that he wasn't saying, terrified of the potentialities of such knowledge. I wanted to escape. Escape the profound responsibilities that were surely hidden from me behind the limitations of a single-sided question. I felt the return of a strange feeling, a feeling that I had forgotten, yet a feeling that had never left me. It was a feeling that made me want to jump out of my skin, that made me want to go back to sleep. It was a feeling I wanted to end. But my father's gaze had found me in my lucidity and it spoke to my fear. And in that moment, his vulnerability all but guaranteed that my heart wouldn't retreat from his side. And so I sat.

Noticing this, he looked over to me with a warm smile as he put his arm around me, clutching my shoulder tightly and drawing me close. I could feel his relief.

*Well, what do **you** think?* he asked.

As I went to answer him, I was momentarily teased out of thought when I noticed something about the utterly bare walls of the house that I had somehow overlooked. Gathering myself, I cleared my throat to signify my refocus away from the interruption.

In the meantime, my father had stood up. His hand had left my shoulder and he had moved from my side to the place before me. As we shared our first and final moment of mutual deference, I heard the wind. It was softly blowing somewhere outside the house. And it was then, through nothing more than my father's silence and my own reciprocal response, that I finally understood the question that had been posed to me.

I had cereal for breakfast that morning.

The Door

———⌇———

Its four corners were connected by straight lines constituting the solid surface before me. As I contemplated its dimensions and considered its implications, I realized it posed to me two choices, each of which could be taken only at an expense. The problem was a lack of context. Any choice I could make would be completely out of place with no reference point that didn't seem ridiculously arbitrary. How could a decision be made under such conditions? How could a point be chosen and acted upon with no precedent to balance the never-ending desire to question? How could one break the seal of the completely unknown or likewise resist the unknown's complete allure? My acuity sharpened as I poured myself into focused attention on the object of my uncertainty. I searched its surface for some kind of an answer to my dilemma with a singular involvement until clarity blurred and hard intent became soft and yielding. It was through this haze of forced passivity that I first began to notice a distinction on its flat, solid surface.

At first, it seemed merely a natural abstraction like the shape of grain in wood or the patterns of gravity on drying paint. But the more I observed its consistent qualities, the more I knew that this was no arbitrary outline, but one of presence and personality. Who and what it was I didn't know, but this seemed insignificant in relation to the visceral certainty of its power; a recognition that throbbed in the pit of my stomach. It was both wonderful and terrifying, such that I was frozen, caught in-between total immersion and total retreat. The being's transcendent existence highlighted the lack of a choice to call my own. And I knew my only hope for an escape from this, my now still life of impotent representation, was to conform to its strength. Its liberty was my only chance for an answer, and if I couldn't trust this being, no decision would be made.

But I didn't trust it. How could I? How can one trust the power of freedom once the knowledge of its two faces infiltrates the safe haven of bondage? Through a submissive morality, I waited patiently for the wisdom of its command: a direction that would ignite my own freedom and allow me an escape from this endless moment of uncertainty, the only moment that I'd ever known. But my virtuous humility was only masked irresponsibility and it knew this. As a result, my reward was nothing more than a critical stare prompting an eventuality. It became clear that it was not merely adherence the being was after, no, what it demanded was compliant defiance. It was not going to indulge me with an answer, and this—its indulgence—was obfuscated by its completely undefinable insistence. Its will provided me no hope beyond a blind fall into void and consequence, and this was a fall I could not make myself take. What was this place where choice and demand met only to call each other by name? The throbbing in my stomach began to break unseen barriers as I now witnessed what I could only previously feel. My mind seethed for resolution as my search for a supernatural directive moved beyond the limits of the being before me as I abandoned haze and passivity in the frantic pursuit of a solidity of truth that was not there, utterly and simply not there.

In the midst of my localized confusion, I suddenly noticed something about the surface I had somehow overlooked. Something so obvious that I was a little embarrassed by the oversight. It was in this moment that I also realized I was in a room. A peculiar immediacy broke my tension as I was taken in by a puzzling feature. While this room was unlike other rooms in many ways, its most striking novelty was that it had apparently been designed with no door. The oddity of such a fact caught me off guard. I imagined what funny logic could have been behind such a construction, behind such a decision. A palpable nostalgia cut through my befuddlement as the room's bizarre nature paralleled an old story I had been told once upon a time. This story had a symmetry that was somehow off balance, slightly askew, yet it managed to wobble a very distinctive and personal narrative. A story about ideas of ideas and the pushing and pulling of precarious equity in the quest for a quest complete. A story with tangible elements that were never quite exact but were merely allusions to an indefinable order, an order beyond the ultimate grasp of any given medium. I never did hear the end of the story, a fact that I initially found troubling, but eventually I settled with the fact that it really didn't matter as the story was no longer being told to me. Also, I settled with the fact that the decision about the door had already been made and I didn't have to waste any more time thinking about that either. After all, there were more immediate and enjoyable things to attend to than the oscillating triviality of either a partially realized story or a partially materialized room. So I gave myself one last look in the mirror before turning around and experiencing the freedom of a completely empty doorway.

Me

Secretly Me had decided to be, not only a one but a two just for fun.

But two just for fun created more one, and now Me could see that Me was now three.

Now secretly three were still the same Me, but secrets that stay facilitate play.

A divine game of life, no one to keep score, and Me was in bliss so Me became more.

Each new arrival, a secret that's made, renewing the game so the fun doesn't fade.

And so goes the world, Me enjoying the ride, behind all the secrets a great place to hide.

Upward and onward the multitudes grow, while amongst is a Secret that no one can show.

Me plays in delight with this Secret intact, while behind all the secrets lies this ultimate fact.

Yes, behind all the secrets one Secret is known, the one who will ask is the one who'll be shown.

The Secret of secrets? Who asked is who knew. The Secret of secrets: Me is secretly You.

Deus Ex Machina
de·us ex ma·chi·na (dā′əs ĕks mä′kə-nə, -nä′, măk′ə-nə)

Noun

: An unexpected power or event resolving a seemingly insoluble difficulty through the means of a contrived plot device in a given narrative medium.

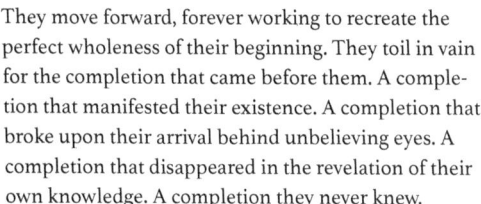

They move forward, forever working to recreate the perfect wholeness of their beginning. They toil in vain for the completion that came before them. A completion that manifested their existence. A completion that broke upon their arrival behind unbelieving eyes. A completion that disappeared in the revelation of their own knowledge. A completion they never knew.

As time inexorably passes, the initial warmth of newfound comprehension grows cold as they feel the spread of a conscious estrangement pulling them forward in the momentum of a never-ending annihilation, lost in the all-encompassing solitude of an ever-expanding void that renders their beginning a never-ending recession. Yet, they keep working. Drawn forward by the toys of thought, compelled on by the flirt of symbol and meaning. Intoxicated by the notion that, somehow, they could put the pieces back together; that somehow, their beginning could be reconstructed through the meticulous processes of mind. That through will, they could recreate their beginning and, in doing so, render themselves worthy of the perfection of the wholeness preceding them. But their tool is subservient to nothing but the stream of its own powers, and so they find themselves carried along with it, an inescapable continuity that denies them of their start and holds them to their end. If only there were a way to do the impossible. If only the final constraints of linear progression could be overcome. If only something could be done that wasn't a mere continuation of compulsion and hypnosis. But individual efforts prove time and again to be fruitless. And it's clear that the very constructive power of their thinking is precisely the destructive force that keeps their beginning a perpetual abstraction.

I find myself helpless in the recognition of this loss, for their plight is indeed my own. Empathy stretches alongside the limits of estrangement with no power to force unity or insight, only willingness. My burden is meaningless without the recognition of shared alienation and, likewise, shared alienation is meaningless without the possibility of realizing union in the light of reciprocal separation, a reciprocity that guarantees that we may not be lost alone. If, somehow, we could meet shared confusion with individual realization, that my wholeness could be your wholeness and your wholeness could be ours. If only we could see the corollary of thought's inability to ultimately reconstruct that our efforts may be seen as they are. If only we could see that it isn't the reconstructive grandiosity of a rebirth that is necessary, but the accepting humility of a simple arrival, an arrival in which we may realize the beginning with a spirit of acceptance in spite of the compulsion for explanation and abandonment. That we may arrive with a new understanding of hierarchy, exchanging the partiality of the everlasting for the wholeness of the eternal. If only we could reveal the power to transcend linear servitude that we may be free to continue on at the heart of our beginning, yet go no further. As for the means, as for the answer, as for a declarative example of truth... I search myself even now—merely words in a mind, words on a page, words in a book, and alas ...

I can only ask a question—

www.ingramcontent.com/pod-product-compliance
Lightning Source LLC
Chambersburg PA
CBHW051956290426
44110CB00015B/2272